Working When You're Not

The business of life between
losing and finding a job

Working When You're Not: The business of life between losing and finding a job
Copyright © 2014 by Dan Schmidt

ALL RIGHTS RESERVED. Printed in the USA.
No part of this book may be reproduced, distributed, or transmitted in any manner—except for brief reviews—or stored in a database or retrieval system, without written permission from the author.

Scripture quotations are taken from the Holy Bible, New International Version®, NIV®. Copyright © 1973, 1978, 1984, 2011 by Biblica, Inc.™
Used by permission of Zondervan. All rights reserved worldwide.

ISBN-13: 978-1503322325
ISBN-10: 1503322327

Cover art by Sharon L. Putt

Working When You're Not

For Paul—
closer than *this* brother?

Inside

1	Deep breath	13
2	Where this book is going	15
3	Who am I to talk…	19
4	Today	23
5	Twenty years from today	27
6	You can't make a mistake	29
7	Willpower is a muscle	31
8	What's the worst that can happen?	33
9	Friends	35
10	Nothing is wasted	39
11	Attacks	41
12	Removal	45
13	The best thing about people screaming at you	47
14	Orange	49
15	The elephant in the foyer	51
16	Excuses	53
17	Invisible	55
18	The next right step	57
19	Time & Money	59
20	Why did you leave?	61
21	Grace	63
22	Dust	65
23	Get to work	69
24	Love	71
25	Weren't we promised jet packs?	75

26	That grain of truth	77
27	Asking questions	79
28	Pop quiz	83
29	Filling the days	85
30	Place holders	89
31	Thunder Mountain	93
32	Dream on	95
33	A prayer to start the day	97
34	Path to great	99
35	Lest we settle	101
36	Hang on	103
37	Facing big problems	105
38	Notice this	107
39	The gallery	109
40	Take a break	111
41	Anxious	113
42	Either/Or	115
43	The way you tell it	117
44	Pushing water uphill	119
45	Worry more	121
46	Don't forget	123
47	Remember	125

Notes	127
Prompts for continued reflection and further discussion	129

1

Deep breath

Have you just lost a job? Have you been looking for several weeks (or months) for a new one?

Wherever you are in this process, let me ask you to pause for a moment and take a deep breath. I'll wait.

Now, take another couple of deep breaths. In, out. In, out.

OK.

Breathing is important because it (1) calms us; and (2) proves that we're still alive. There's a third gift connected with breathing, available to those whose lives lean toward God: it reminds us of the Spirit, who is described as not only wind, but also breath. God breathes, we can recall when we draw air into our lungs, and when God breathes, all sorts of good happens.

When a job ends, we can panic, or clench up—and if that happens, we stop breathing, or draw only small sips of air. Exactly what we need in such times—oxygen so that our brains function, so that our blood moves—we cut off. We tighten, get small, hunker down.

So breathe.

And as you breathe, remember that while some things have changed, others haven't. For instance, God hasn't left the building. There are still some people who love you.

Breathe.

Because here, in this place that can or will look desolate, there is work to do. You may not receive an income for it; it may not advance your career in any predictable way—but it is work all the same, as you reflect on what occurred, figure out how to navigate the days ahead, and prepare for what's next. And to do this work, you need to

breathe.

2

Where this book is going

This is not primarily a *How-to* book—so you won't find a lot on constructing a killer résumé or dressing for the interview. That said, I will occasionally toss in a few tips acquired along the way about the job search process.

It doesn't deal much with the matter of vocation, either. While I firmly believe that vocation is important, my experience is also that it can change. But I'm not addressing this issue in any organized way here.

Another thing this book doesn't do: it doesn't talk much about conduct in the marketplace. There are important discussions about what it takes to be a good boss or employee—but those are in books written by other people.

For the most part, the book you're holding will examine, consider, and reflect on the space between losing and finding a job. To that end, a series of short chapters will deal with what I and other travelers on this road have encountered.

And just so you know, these chapters are not clumped by particular topics so much as in a loose orbit around the central idea of dealing with life 'in between'. Also, when chapters are quoting outside sources, or sparking more thoughts, they'll be marked with a ▶.

I'd suggest you try reading no more than a couple of entries at a sitting, and that you give yourself a few moments to digest what you're reading. There's usually space on or near each page where you can scratch notes, or questions, or exclamation points, too—and you may find that aids in processing this experience. If you're someone who prefers to do this sort of thing in the company of others, you'll find several 'Discussion Prompts' near the end of this book to nudge that along.

Remember: while it can feel like you're on your own in this time, there are probably others nearby who understand and can empathize. They might be going through the same thing, or have it in their background. Or they might just be willing to walk with you during this season. Indeed, it may be that some will read this book not because they're in between, but so they can better understand what someone next door, at church, or across the country is facing. Connections like these, however they occur, are critical at times like this.

Let me also add, by way of introduction, that I'm commenting on this 'in between' season as a Christian who counts on God's knowledge, power, love, grace, and peace—and for whom the Bible is a go-to source of wisdom and encouragement. And while I think other Christians will resonate with that perspective, I also recognize that a person doesn't have to be a Christian—or much of a Christian—to enter the discussion about or benefit from reflection on what happens after losing, but before finding, a job.

3

Who am I to talk…

… or write about the space between losing and finding a job?

Some background:
My first full-time job—after a series of part-time gigs during high school, college, and grad school—started a few years into our marriage. A church hired me, and my boss wanted weekly reports of how I spent my time—broken out in quarter-hour segments.

In my two years there, I was a ping pong ball being smacked between different constituencies; I left feeling rather battered. We moved east, to another church. This one was going to sponsor me in planting a new church, and in the months leading up to that, I met with its leaders nearly every week over pancakes at Denny's. Casual, encouraging—this group was very different from the one I'd left. They wanted to talk about what was going on, what was on the horizon. Ten months later, with ten people (my wife, me, our two toddlers, and six others), we bounced from that safe place into a dozen years of the grit and glory that is church planting. Along the way, I got to help some people, got to learn from some people, and got yelled at by some people. In my recollection, the last of these was not the least common.

Church work threw me into the deep end, fully clothed and partly conscious. That I survived the passive-aggressive leadership, poor communication, cultural puzzles, interpersonal anguish, theological conundrums, and financial uncertainty so typical in that environment is a testimony to God's empowering, and the encouragement of friends and family. That I could imagine during that time no career other than "full-time ministry" makes me a resolute believer in grace.

More pastoring followed. One of those positions required moving overseas; I got fired eleven months later. We limped back to the states and holed up in a tiny condo. I wrote a book there, but otherwise did not have steady employment over the next year. Then another international job opened up. We went, and I suffered from whiplash in the first few months, wondering when something unexpected was going to smack me. But nothing did. A two-year contract stretched to three, and then we parted company upon realizing we needed to deal with kids and college and Alzheimer's. We left, but without the prospect of another job. Several months passed before I began a stint with a mission agency that had me on the road or in the air two or three weeks a month. Then, another church.

During more than three decades and more than one career, I've had several jobs but not much job security. Compensation varied, and arrived in different ways, too: regular salary, raised support, supplemental income (i.e. second, third jobs), unexpected gifts, a drawing down of savings. I got fired, down-sized, had a contract terminated prematurely, and negotiated an amicable parting. In just over thirty years of "full-time ministry," I've answered to eight different employers in three states and two foreign countries. I've also been out of work (that is, with no regular job or income) for close to twenty-four months.

Funny, though, that while my experience is unusual, it's far from unique. A lot of people get bounced around in their jobs; a lot of us get fired, or let go, or mistreated. Like others, I know what it's like to be in a job you love, to be in a position you can't wait to leave, to draw a generous paycheck, and to wonder how you'll pay some bills.

So this 'in-between' space—I've been there. In fact, as I'm writing this, I'm there now. With this book, I'm joining others who occupy a similar place, and wanting us to think about what's going on here. I've noticed heads nodding when I've shared my story in different venues; something similar might happen as folks turn these pages. My hope is that talking about what we've been through—what some of us are going through right now—will bring a little light to what can be a dark and cloudy time, and remind those who might be feeling isolated that we do not have to do this alone.

I'm also hoping that in the ebb and flow of our jobs—in and out of those seasons which Ecclesiastes describes so vividly—we will find ways to manage all we face so that the God we cherish (and yes, the God who sometimes sends us down this path) gets glory.

4

Today

The college I attended had a motto we heard from time to time: *Not somehow, but triumphantly*. It was meant to remind us that while life can be tough, there are ways through. And not just any old way. Life on a higher plane was desirable, the motto taught us—and possible. Like any motto, it was pithy (short enough for a bumper sticker) and powerful (it resonated with what many of us want to be true). And like many mottoes, it also offered a way forward that was, to be honest, out just a little past the reach of many. To say it another way, while sayings like this can motivate, they can also produce guilt.

More of this we do not need, especially in the liminal space between losing and finding a job. As those who have spent any time here already know, this in between place is a breeding ground for guilt. For instance, "What did you do today?" is no longer an innocent, throwaway question: When one is out of work, it has a sharper edge. Hours that once zipped by faster than Barry Allen now pass at a glacial rate. And what about the emotional cast of this season? Snow White's bluebirds fill the room one morning, and people have to ask you to stop whistling. But on other afternoons or evenings, the dreary Mountains of Mordor can feel awfully near.

So: how do you get through these days?

You can look for people who will cheer you up (and not those who, having seen cumulus nimbus hovering over you for some time, give you a wide berth).

You can binge-watch shows that, in others settings, you would not consider. A variation on this is doing something you would not otherwise do (i.e. it had been previously avoided not because you were too busy, but because it had no redeeming value).

There's food. And/or whine. Or,

How about grabbing a book or a shovel or a mixing bowl and doing your best to hang on while it's still daylight? Then, go to bed early and trust that tomorrow will be better.

Two other ideas:

1. Give yourself permission to have bad (or at least, cloudy) days.

2. Pat yourself on the back for making it through such days—not triumphantly, maybe, but somehow.

5

Twenty years from today

When you look back on this episode in your life, how will you remember it?

Were you courageous? Fearful?
Were you overwhelmed by the past or the future?
Did you notice what was happening around you in the moment?
Did you discover a new interest? Make a new friend?
Were you kind to yourself? Were you hard on yourself?
Looking back, would you go through it again if you had the choice? Really?

A lot of the story about this time is yours to write.

6

You can't make a mistake

An issue of the alumni magazine from a seminary I attended noted the passing of a beloved professor. The magazine reported on the memorial service, including a remembrance from one of the professor's daughters in which she recalled a conversation between the two of them.

The young woman was at a crossroads. Several options were in front of her, and she was confused about which to pick. Did her father have any wisdom? Could he shed light on her dilemma? Would he tell her what to do?

Offered a setup like that by one of my own kids, I would probably lay out a couple of well-conceived courses of action and then expect one or the other to be followed. This prof, however, took a different path. "You can't make a mistake," he told his daughter.

At first, she's confused by this advice, because it doesn't answer the question she'd posed. She wanted specifics; she got fortune cookie. But then, she realizes that her father has given her a gift. And as she explained to those gathered for the funeral, he'd been giving her gifts like this for a long time—words of grace and wisdom coupled with training in the ways of God, who expects, gives, and forms faith in His kids. Her dad was telling her to lean into that. And when someone who loves you, someone you respect, someone who knows stuff thinks you can't make a mistake? Talk about a confidence booster.

Today—or yesterday, or next week—various possibilities are spooling out in front of you. In all likelihood, no one of them has a blinking light attached, to indicate that it is THE right/best/most obvious choice. So: is God in the mix? Is your brain switched on?

You can't make a mistake.

7

Willpower is a muscle

People who study such things tell us that willpower is a muscle which can be exercised, and, like any muscle, weakened. So if, for instance, we keep choosing to be positive, if we've sent out a job application (or three) and had no (favorable or otherwise) response, if we've tried to stay at our desks and keep plugging away at the resume, or cover letter, or the reading we need to do to learn new stuff—after activity like this, our willpower is worn out. We get tired. We might even get a bit grumpy.

Either of these can affect us; they're both likely to have an effect on those we're around, too. So it helps to have a strategy for dealing with a weakened will. That way, we're more likely to finish a day with a sense of accomplishment. We also won't have added new reasons for feeling guilty.

This strategy? Here are some possibilities...

Set a time for bringing each day's activity to a close. It's easy to think you should keep going, keep pushing. But more effort doesn't automatically produce better results.

Make sure a nearby basket/drawer/box/shelf is stocked with healthy snacks. Consume as often as necessary.

Exercise. Walk, bike, swim, or run for twenty to thirty minutes a day, four, five, six times a week. (Am I sounding like your mom?)

Understand the connection between tired and stupid—and set up warning signals that tell you when you're passing the former on the way to the latter.

Expect to get tired. You're in a sprint. You're in a marathon. Sometimes they both happen on the same day. You're working, remember?

Make a chart to keep in a desk drawer and each day you do well, give yourself a tiny gold star.

If you feel yourself starting to slip, pray. "O God, help!" is really good, and never gets old.

And one more thing, about feeling guilty: if you haven't done anything wrong, you're not.

8

What's the worst that can happen?

One of my friends is a philosopher. His brain wraps around ideas I don't really understand, and his grasp of arcane concepts is impressive. He's also something of an expert about getting stuff done: because he has so many ideas, and wants to accomplish a great deal, he's devised ways of tackling long lists of tasks. His success rate is impressive, too.

I heard him explaining one of his strategies for getting to done; it went something like this:

> If I have a task to accomplish but then start to get bothered by the possibility of failure, or find myself worrying over how others might react to what I'm doing, I ask, *What's the worst that can happen?* I let myself face this, and then decide: Would I be OK with that? If yes, I continue. If not, I pause to make an adjustment.

My own tendency, upon encountering options and pondering reactions is to think about possible outcomes and then... do nothing. So my friend's approach definitely has the advantage of encouraging forward progress. And I've tried it a couple of times, with good effect. (I realized after hearing him talk about this that I'd used a version of his approach when I was traveling a lot. Despite many hours in airplanes, I tended to be a nervous passenger—until I hit upon the idea of imagining, as we were taxiing down the runway, that the plane would explode upon takeoff. When that didn't happen, I could enjoy the rest of the trip.)

Regarding the task before you right now that feels so enormous, what's the worst outcome you can imagine? Can you live with that?

For extra bonus points, can you imagine a good outcome? Could you live with *that*?

9

Friends

When you're in between, friends are essential.

Yes, things with friends at such times can get odd. While they're 'at work', you're home in front of the computer, wearing sweats, eating scones (of course, you're looking at job notices, but still). They go to office Christmas parties; you drink eggnog in your living room. They plan vacations; you check the credit card statements every few days. They can get worried for you; you—wait a minute: this is something you both share!

But, if being out of and looking for work is like climbing a mountain, trying to occupy the space between jobs on your own is crossing the Andes in a swimsuit.

Friends are of inestimable value during this season—even if they're not in the immediate neighborhood. So by all means, reach out. Let your friends know what's going on (my friend Rich told me about a guy he knew who was looking for more than a year. He sent updates every month or two so those further afield could keep track of his situation). Tap friends for things you need—whether it's carpentry or legal advice. Would your friends contact *their* friends about your job search?

Something else to bring up with your friends: Ask them to come find you if you disappear for a few days. This withdrawal can happen, but if your friends are in the loop, you won't go unnoticed for long.

Asking is tough, right? It's like admitting you're needy, that you can't do everything on your own. Exactly. But remember: This was true even when you had a job. It's just that then, you had more insulation.

Prepare to encourage your friends, too. It's weird, I know, but you being out of work makes them uncomfortable. They feel awkward; they wish things were different for you. You can sink into this, and widen any small crack that presents itself into a full-blown whine—but try not to let that happen. And don't let them complain on your behalf, either. Bear in mind that while friends can sharpen one another, or sand down rough edges, they don't poke holes. Friends lift one another; they pour strength into each other.

So agree with your friends to look up more than to look back, or to look down.

If your friend shares your faith, remind that person of prayer's efficacy. Tell him or her how you've sensed God's strength; share a story about some unexpected event or development that reminded you that God is still vitally interested in your well-being. Offer to pray for your friend, too.

One more suggestion—which will require some advance thinking. When a friend says, "I wish I could do more…," have a strong, true, faith-building, sincere reply that raises both you and your friend just a little bit above the fray.

10

Nothing is wasted

When I was in elementary school, my mom planted marigolds in our front yard garden and at the end of the season when the flower petals dropped off, I put the seeds that remained in envelopes and sold them to neighbors. When sales slowed, I switched to construction. Our back yard had a small creek where I built forts on stilts using lumber scavenged from new homes going up down the block.

As a teenager, I delivered newspapers, mowed grass, washed and waxed Cessnas at a local airfield. I joined the school newspaper and yearbook staff. I cooked for youth group retreats.

During college I painted houses and took pictures for a local newspaper. In grad school, I waited tables and watched houses. I copied and filed clippings for a private library. I figured out how to research and became a Latin tutor (OK, this was a reach: friends had a kid in school who was struggling and they knew I was a student of dead languages. Could I help? they wondered. Sure, I thought—all I had to do was stay one step ahead of an eighth grader.). I learned word-processing on a Mac Plus (check Google, or a museum) at the public library.

In my 'professional' career? I pastored small churches, some of which used old buildings that needed paint and other remodeling. When I wasn't pastoring (that is, when I had been fired, or let go, or left), I fell back on catering and restaurant work. I wrote books and articles. I edited other people's writing. I mowed lawns. When finances were lean (did I mention I was a pastor?), I returned to my scavenger ways.

What did you used to do—back when the stakes weren't as high, back when work was more of a lark? What did you learn? What stayed with you?

Could you use that now? And even if you can't do exactly the same thing as before (like door-to-door sales, or setting up a lemonade stand), what might be transferable from those younger days?

11

Attacks

If you're walking in the way of Jesus, you already know something about the rich treasures of that life. Chances are also good that by this point, you've experienced challenges to staying on this path, too. You know you have an Advocate; you've also encountered enemies.

By "enemies," I'm not referring to (or even suggesting) those at the office/school/hospital/church/warehouse/etc. who did you wrong, so much as the cosmic forces arrayed against God's own. The apostle Paul refers to this bunch in Ephesians 6, reminding us about a struggle that pits us not against flesh and blood, but against spiritual foes.

Here's the bad news, based on the warning Paul delivers: You should expect attacks. And here's worse news: Expect these attacks to come when you are tired, stretched, and already having a terrible, no good, very bad day.

The enemies Paul describes are not known for their manners; they don't wait until we're ready before mounting a sortie against us. Rather, they fall on us when we're weak, or they slink in when we're otherwise occupied. They create confusion, revel in disorder, and promote misunderstanding. Whatever strengthens community and good will, they oppose.

Like the day I was sitting at my desk, mulling recent events. It came to mind that my wife had said and done some things that undermined me. Further, she had not helped when help was needed, had not been attentive at key moments. My frustration grew.

I should confront her, I thought. *This needs to stop! After all...*

Another voice in my brain was putting up a protest. "This is not the way of my wife," that part of my brain was saying, in a tinny, somewhat muffled voice. "She is consistently patient, encouraging, cheerful, kind. She makes really good scones, too."

But, I sputtered. *What about—?*

The other voice offered no rebuttal. Instead, it took a different tack. "You're not right in your assessment, but you are under siege. A hostile force is attempting to dismantle the peace in your home, the love between you and her."

Oh.

12

Removal

So I had this idea that scared me.

I found myself wondering if employees ever need to be removed from the space they've been filling. Up until that idea bushwhacked me, I was pretty much assuming that while I needed the particular job I had, the arrangement was reciprocal: The job needed me, too.

But what if that's not the case?

What if, from time to time, those in various positions (maybe—especially?—positions of leadership) need to be set aside for a spell?

Perhaps this notion has merit, I was willing to concede (I wasn't *eager* to concede, you understand)—but only if some good might come of that setting aside.

Like teaching the person in that position that s/he wasn't essential? Like showing those who relied on that person/position that there are others ways of coping?

As I say, this was a terrifying idea.

13

The best thing about people screaming at you

Has someone—or maybe several someones—really let you have it? Maybe it was in your face or behind your back; a ground-swallowing explosion or a slow drip on your forehead; a carefully orchestrated marshalling of evidence or a smear campaign. Whatever happened, however it went down, you got flattened.

And then, you left that place, where that happened. You licked your wounds, told your story, tried to make sense of it, got your faith realigned, saw some professionals, took up yoga or bread-making or marathons—and then, you found another job. Which went great until you saw headlights in your windshield and knew what was coming at you full throttle.

This time, what happened?

In *Star Trek VI*, when several of the crew are, once again, in deep trouble, Scotty blurts out, "We're dead!" This makes those around him shudder. All, that is, except for Spock, who is nonplussed. What's the difference between the first officer and the chief engineer? "I've been dead before," Spock says.

If you've already gone through the worst possible outcome and lived to tell the tale—well, the next time something really awful is rears its ugly head, you're more likely to yawn. Been there, done that, got the scars to prove it, you can say.

Perhaps in this season, while you're out of work, you'll be newly empowered by the memory of resurrection?

14

Orange

This book's cover features a piece of art created by my friend Sharon. When Sharon was young, she was an artist. Then she wasn't (life got serious; art is frivolous). Then things went south in some arenas and Sharon needed a different focus. Art happened.

The original hangs in my study. I like the color, the energy, the ethos of this painting. It brightens the room. It also reminds me that life doesn't stand still, that we rarely do the same thing every day over the course of a lifetime.

A relationship that should have lasted fades; a career full of promise stalls out. What then?

We paint.

15

The elephant in the foyer

When you do get an interview, or an opportunity to talk with someone who might be able to move the chains a bit, it's possible that you will give vent to what's bubbling inside you—that the wrongs you've been done, the ways you've been sidelined, the hopes you've been pinning, the queues in which you've been standing, the insecurity you've been feeling, the boredom of endless days without meaningful activity, the anger at all sorts of stuff—all that will boil over in the course of this conversation.

Don't let that happen.

Keep that elephant in the foyer; don't let it walk into the room with you and your prospective boss. In that place, with that person, it is a new day, and you are interacting with someone who does not know—and does not need to know—the anguish you carry because of what happened somewhere else.

Start fresh. Maybe, start over. But don't dig into the past and pull out that bag of peanuts. Because once you open it, the mess just gets bigger.

16

Excuses

Yes, I'm grumpy. But you would be, too, if you'd just been fired, or were out of work.

Let's parse this.

1. *Yes, I'm grumpy.*
Apparently I'm still in community. People notice me, call me out, and I'm willing—right now, at least—to agree with their assessment.

2. *But*
At the same time, I recognize the danger of the community losing its patience, so I hustle to explain myself. An adversarial like "but" allows me to acknowledge the grumpiness. Then, it dismantles that assessment with an explanation that justifies the attitude without apologizing for it in any way. *But* even gives the attitude a place at the community table.

3. *too*
We're all in this together, right? So there's no need for you to be so harsh. And, by the way,

while I might be the grumpy one today, tomorrow, it might be you.

4. *if*
Conditional clauses (*if ... then*) are logical powerhouses. Even if I leave out the *then* part, it's pretty clear that I'm making a rational argument here: "*if* you'd been fired, *then* you'd be grumpy." And logic is good, right?

5. *fired ... out of work*
Having used a rational argument, I now appeal to the emotions by shifting attention from my attitude to my circumstances. Circumstances which are, by any measurement, grievous. Further, people going through what I'm experiencing naturally/normally/understandably/always react with grumpiness, or something akin to it. This should not be unexpected by those around me; indeed, those around me should be inclined to give me a pass when it comes to sour attitudes.

Success! In two sentences I've accounted for and justified my foul mood. But: What good—for me, for those around me—has come of this?

17

Invisible

Why don't they see me?

I'm the right person for this job—why can't s/he understand this? Why don't they call? Why doesn't someone seek me out? Am I that easy to forget?

On several occasions, I've spotted what looks like a good situation. Scratch that: it was *perfect*. I dropped into high gear, sent my paperwork, made the calls, sat by the phone, got my hopes up. And then ... nothing. For a while, I was crestfallen.

But then—and sometimes, it took a few months, or maybe a year—I'd look back at what had seemed so perfect. From that vantage point, I'd find myself thinking, *Sheesh!* I sure am glad I don't have that job. Meaning, that perfect job I didn't get.

Sour grapes? Nope. More like broad daylight shining on that job and my life, illuminating the fact that the two didn't fit together very well. And, that I'd even been saved some heartache. What I couldn't see at the time became, a bit later, more clear.

These days, I'm a little less put out when the perfect job doesn't materialize. I'm also trying not to have to wait a few weeks/months/years before appreciating what didn't happen. I'm even a little easier with being invisible.

18

The next right step

We need to think about goals.

At least, this is what people—well-meaning people—around us insist. Problem is, while there is something exhilarating about setting a goal, there's something exhausting about trying to reach it.

Not only that, but achieving a goal—like, say, getting a job—is not always entirely in our hands. Often, what we're after depends on someone else stepping in to make a decision, write a check, or change a preference.

There's an art (and, some would argue, a science) to encouraging this sort of action. But if our goal depends too much on what others must do, we may be waiting a long time before it's realized.

Instead, how about we direct thought and energy to what we're capable of doing? What if we focus on what we can influence?

Goals have their place, but maybe today's question is not *When will* (or, *why doesn't*) this *happen?* but rather, *What can I do now?*

19

Time & Money

When we are gainfully employed, we draw a paycheck and then must decide what to do with the money. Some (most?) is already spoken for, but there are usually a few bucks we get to spend as we please. To say it another way, jobs that pay us often give us more income than we need. The trick in that sort of situation is figuring out what to do with a surplus of funds.

When we no longer have those jobs, however, this extra money vanishes. In fact, one of the real stresses at such times is brought on by the reduction of income. Interestingly, this is also a season when, because the demands of a paying job have evaporated, we have more time. Now, we need to figure out what to do with a surplus of hours.

20

Why did you leave?

How you answer this question is likely to affect at least some of what you do next.

If you were forced out against your will, or before you had planned to go, you'll probably need to deal with some resentment.

If the parting was ugly—you were falsely accused, the terms of your contract were ignored, you had no opportunity for rebuttal or explanation—you'll probably feel resentment *and* may need some professional assistance (an attorney, a counselor, a spiritual director).

If this was an anticipated change, on account of family issues, or another 'call', or because you just felt done, you'll want to focus on a smooth transition. This starts with good communication well ahead of the decision to leave—so if that didn't occur, start there: Apologize as needed, and get matters cleared up.

21

Grace

On days when I'm feeling beat up and not good for a whole lot? It helps to remember that grace effects a repurposing of what's lost, broken, discarded, or old. A repurposing, let it be said, that brings delight.

22

Dust

When my friend Keith heard I'd been let go, he asked a few questions about the circumstances, and how I was feeling. Then he told me I needed to move on. "Shake the dust off your feet," he said. A few weeks later, I read the same phrase in a piece about job transitions from a writer I respect and enjoy.

When I hear the same thing coming at me from different directions, I tend to sit up and take notice.

Both Keith and this writer were quoting Jesus, who was preparing disciples for their first missionary foray. Here's the context:

> Whatever house you enter, stay there until you leave that town. If people do not welcome you, leave their town and shake the dust off your feet as a testimony against them.
> (*Luke 9:4-5; see also Matt 10:12-15 and Mark 6:10-11*)

That Jesus instructs this dust-shaking exercise is curious, since He is generally known for patience and long-suffering. Indeed that general tendency of His may explain why all three Synoptic Gospels report the saying: They want to stress that Jesus really meant it.

But how do you know when it's time to knock on doors, and when it's time to move on—minus the dust from that place, of course?

Seems like there's a clue in how Jesus sets this up. He encourages disciples to go to these new places and seek out those willing and ready to welcome them. If such folk can't be found, well, then: Off with their dust! It's not, however, that disciples should be eager to quit that town. Rather, they're meant to go, to do what they can to stay, to be open to a welcome being extended. And then, if that's not forthcoming, a de-dusting ensues.

How does this fit when it comes to the workplace? Maybe like this: You go, you pour yourself in to the tasks at hand, you try to fit in with what's going on and being asked. But then, the day comes when your presence is no longer required or desired. Some conversations might ensue. There might be opportunity for negotiation, or renegotiation. But also, maybe not. And once it's clear that you are *persona non grata*, you go.

You don't look back, you don't whine, you don't wish it was different, you don't even badmouth the ~~idiots~~ people who let you go. And, you leave with nothing from that place that doesn't belong to you—not a desk chair, not a mouse pad, not even dust from the shop floor.

You are not, however, only leaving. For in the departing lies the implication that you are going somewhere else. Sooner or later, you'll find that place where you will be welcomed, where what you bring is exactly what they want. ▸

23

Get to work

This is an imperative, right? And by now you have probably heard the command issued in a booming voice, or by a looming boss—the latest in a series of directions that have been pressing in on you, weighing you down.

But what if it's an invitation—part of a collaboration involving you and people you love (or at least can tolerate) who are, like you, motivated, creative, eager?

Or a sign over the portal to a wide, bright field (rather than a narrow, low-ceilinged room where you sit—never near a window—for yet another day of drudgery)?

Or an expression of privilege, as in: Today, we get to work! After all, work is not a given, and no matter how much we might feel we are entitled to a job, or something profitable/meaningful to do, there is no guarantee this will happen. The universe (or, our country, or our culture, or…) does not owe us.

Interpretations like these crack open soul-enriching ways to think about getting to work. We remember, for instance, that not all we call "work" is salaried. Indeed, if we worked only for money, would that create a world we'd want to inhabit?

24

Love

One of Jesus' more disturbing ideas is "Love your enemies" (this shows up in a couple of place—like, for example, Matthew 5:44).

Enemies who live a time zone or ocean away are one thing; people like this become generic enough that we can muster love for them without too much effort. But the enemies Jesus seems to have in mind are much closer. They are in your neighborhood, at your church, in your home.

Have you had the experience of people promising something—not just something you'd like, but something you, or the job you're doing, or the task you've been assigned, needs—only to have them back out? Did you grow up with the injunction to "respect your elders" and then find yourself working with or for elders who were anything but worthy of respect? Has your character been impugned? Have accusations been made against you? Were you laid low by stress because others just wouldn't help?

The people on the other side of these pressures, challenges, disappointments, and difficulties: they're the enemy.

Love *them*?

Like a lot of people in my profession, I'm conflict-averse. This is lamentable, because in my profession, conflict is common. Part of the problem stems from the tendency among those in 'people-helping' professions to be 'people-pleasers' who are reluctant to do anything that might upset others. Strange, how we gravitate to the very work that includes a large chunk of what we're not inclined to do very well.

I have, by sheer dint of practice, become better at dealing with conflict. In part, I have one of my jobs to thank for this, since the first couple of years in that position were mostly a matter of putting out fires and dealing with difficult people. But there's been another factor helping me improve: the realization that the way I go into conflict—the way I confront—matters.

If I remain fearful of the outcome, or resistant to the process, little of good is likely to occur. On the other hand, if I can find a way to take Jesus' words about loving enemies to heart, then what looks like conflict and confrontation takes on a different hue. Not only that, but if I'm able to surrender my need for a pristine reputation (not that I'm careless about my behavior, but rather that I'm indifferent to opinion) and allow myself to imagine what a healed relationship looks like, or the gains if what we're working on comes to pass, then I find myself ready—even eager—for the confrontation required by the conflict that has occurred.

This all sounds very nice.

But here's the shocker: It can happen. And I say this on the basis of personal (and repeated) experience: I find myself facing a problem, which is caused by or connected with particular people; my initial reaction is fear, or anger, or anxiety, or some blend thereof; Jesus' words, brought to mind, no doubt, by the Spirit, wedge into the cracks and expand; I pray for love; love arrives; I go; we talk; things change.

Sadly, the outcome isn't always positive, and I don't always walk away with a relationship restored or even intact. But then, the beauty of Jesus' command is that it's not outcome-dependent. That is, we're not told to love *so that*.... Rather, we're simply told to love.

In doing this, we side with God, who loves this same crazy way. What follows—well, that depends on several factors. The live question for me—for you—is: Will we love? And when we do, a whole new bunch of possibilities emerge.

25

Weren't we promised jet packs?

We had a bright, shiny future all mapped out. People told us what they saw in us, from us, because of us. It sounded wonderful.

Then, *this* happened. Given all the options before us, this outcome was not among those we had considered. It was definitely not what we had imagined. We hadn't even thought it possible.

There must be some mistake.

Sometimes, that's exactly the problem—someone goofs up and we get caught in the gears. Sometimes, though, the predictions are just wrong. Our expectations are not always based in reality.

And sometimes, there was no mistake.

I heard someone talk about 'calling', especially as it related to a calling from God. I can't remember right now who said this (if it was you, let me know and I'll add a note on the back page), but the person's point was that when you look at those whom God called, you often find that (a) they weren't all that keen on God's idea for their life, and (b) what they were called into was far from easy or straightforward. This person went on to ask whether we ought to be talking about calling with the level of enthusiasm that is often on display.

Have you been called to something—like plumbing, or sculpting, or preaching, or home-making, or lawyering, or dancing, or wrapping tape around athletes' limbs? If so, you may be in for a wilder ride than the brochures promised regarding the arena you entered.

Maybe you've discovered that already.

26

That grain of truth

Were you taught, like I was, that in every criticism there is a grain of truth?

I've been criticized a lot (I'm not proud of this, but there it is), and I've spent a lot of time ruminating on the negative words spoken to or about me. In large measure, I did this because I had been told that such comments were educational. I would find in them—somewhere—something that would be good for my character, and beneficial for my future.

Sometimes, this was true.

Like during college, when I had a job as a resident assistant in a dorm. I was supposed to do some stuff at the end of the school year, but instead, I left without making sure my responsibilities had been taken care of. My boss wrote me a letter about that, taking me to task. His criticism held more than a grain of truth.

But sometimes, it is not.

I've also been on the receiving end of those who thought I needed to do/stop/change something, and then lit into me about my shortcomings. On such occasions, I've followed the lead of King Hezekiah, spreading the letter I've received or recounting the speech I've heard before God (see the story in 2 Kings 19:14). Is this me? I ask. When it's not, I put the letter away (and typically, if that letter is unsigned, I put it far away) and don't let it get traction in my brain.

Sometimes, this grain is far smaller than a mustard seed, and no good fruit grows out of it.

27

Asking questions

Changes like losing a job create opportunities for reflection and self-examination. They do more than this, to be sure, but rarely less. So, take some time to ask questions that might otherwise have been pushed into a closet under the stairs—like:

Are you (still) in the right field?
You might be assuming that what has happened is a temporary glitch—that you'll be back in the saddle of another similar horse very soon. Maybe. But try taking a moment for something wild and crazy: Ask yourself if, given the opportunity, you would do something different. What tumbles out of your response?

Would the way(s) you handle yourself in the marketplace benefit from adjustment?
This is a polite means of inquiring about how you speak in public, deal with problems, face conflict, organize your time, interact with people, handle money—you get the idea. Trouble is, answering this question requires taking stock of attitudes, behavior, and tendencies in conversa-

tion—and this can be tricky to do for ourselves. That's when having a trusted friend who would give it to you straight and love you no matter what helps. Can you seek the counsel of such a person?

Are there other indicators—say, past letters or comments—that dovetail with what you heard at the exit interview or when your boss let you know your time was up? Can you accept what these critiques surfaced? And then, as far as actually making the changes, there are probably books to read, people to talk with, mentors to imitate, and so on. What will it take to put yourself where that can happen?

What about learning new skills?
Did your job end because you couldn't do what was expected, or couldn't adjust to new demands? Any chance you were a victim of success (that is, your good work created a situation you were not equipped to handle)? As you ponder these possibilities, might you also consider using the time you suddenly have in abundance to pick up or sharpen some skills?

During one season of being between jobs, I got serious about editing and formatting. After working on various books and articles of my own, I realized that if I helped others who wanted to write, I could generate some income. So I researched, practiced, hung out a shingle, and made contact with writers' groups in churches wanting to produce a collection of essays. It was fun; it padded our accounts, too. And, it gave me a transportable skill I can bring to wherever I land and use with those who want to express themselves, but need additional encouragement to do so.

::

You can want to go back to what you were doing—and you may. But in this moment when what's next is not plain, you have an opportunity to look down a few other corridors.

Is this a time to transition not only to a different job, but maybe a different career?

What about moving across town, across state, across an ocean?

Are you ready to step out on your own? Would you prefer to have someone else assume some or all of the risk you've been carrying until now? There are a bunch of important questions that deserve to be asked when you're in between.

28

Pop quiz

1. What are you afraid of?
Check as many items below as are relevant:

___ being powerless and out of control
___ looking needy
___ no one will hire me
___ friends will get sick of my pain
___ getting left behind because I can't afford to go shopping, or dinner, or to take a trip to the shore
___ other (specify:)

2. Why do you think "Fear not!" is one of the Bible's most common commands?

3. If you could dismiss fear from your life, would you? Why/why not?

Extra credit: plan a strategy for overcoming one of the fears that currently occupies space in your heart (e.g. enlist a friend's help; pray; say something like: "In the cold light of day, this fear makes less sense than rugby.")

29

Filling the days

One of the things about having a job is that you don't have to worry about how you'll occupy your waking hours. When you're out of work, though, this changes.

Now the days are yours to fill. What will go into them?

There's looking for the next job, of course, which is no small task. As my brother (who also has experience with this in between time) said the first time I was out of work, looking for a job *is* a job. Admittedly, the pay for this job is low and the benefit package non-existent, but otherwise, the insight is sound. It takes work to find work.

You probably already know this. In fact, you may find yourself getting a little tired of this particular job. To prepare a résumé, send it out, and wait; to discover that often all your hard work in finding an opening and expressing interest is met by … nothing—this can be tough.

Perhaps it will help to consider what you're doing while this is your job, and also what you're learning.

First, what you're doing. You are putting yourself out; you are making your interest known. There will be some well-meaning folk who urge you to "be patient" and "wait on the Lord"—and while both of these are surely important, you also grasp that God is not often in the business of making someone you do not know or have not met pick up the phone and call you. Doing something does not imply that you are no longer trusting the Lord.

Second, what you're learning. Crafting a résumé, writing a cover letter, talking with a prospective employer—all of these call for skill, and very little goes especially well the first or second time you try. Expect to prepare a better résumé after you've sent your fifteenth application; expect that your cover letter three months into the search will be more clear, more succinct, more focused. Once you've talked with several prospects, the quiver in your voice is likely to diminish. You won't give up as easily, either, nor will you realize ten minutes after you hung up that you should have added that pertinent detail about your experience. You'll have figured out how to get the person on the other end to ask another question;

you'll be more practiced in extending the conversation once you've made that initial connection.

In this job—the one where you're looking—you're doing and learning a lot. ▶

30

Place holders

You find what looks like the perfect position, and you dash off an application with the confidence of an old hand. A day or two passes during which you imagine yourself in that job, filing that role, drawing that paycheck, living in that city. There's a spring in your step, and your spirits soar.

Then an email comes, or a letter, explaining that while you certainly have much to offer, there have been numerous inquiries, and those responsible for the hire are going to give you a pass. Does the air go out of your balloon?

For a minute or two or ten, yes—and this is normal. This job would have been ideal! But you're not going to get the chance to see it come to pass, and now you have a choice. You can sink into despair. Or, you can, as *The Princess Bride*'s Westley advised Inigo Montoya, get used to disappointment.

These two sound similar, but they're not. The first option goes to a dark place—what *Pilgrim's Progress* memorably described as the Slough of Despond. The second, though: this one can build a muscle. Because not everything you try (or want) is going to work out. And don't imagine I'm saying this simply because I'm a melancholic pessimist.

OK, it's true: my personality does lean toward melancholy, and all things being equal, for me the glass is typically half empty. But I'd rather describe myself as realistic. That is, I'd like to point out, to myself and others, that the first opening one pursues rarely pans out. If we manage, however, to make room in our hearts and brains for some measure of disappointment, we'll be better able to press on and keep searching.

And what's really interesting is to back up a moment and consider how you felt when you first saw that job you thought you'd like. Do you remember the delight in discovering it? Do you recall how it felt to imagine yourself in that chair, behind that desk, on that floor?

You can hold that. You can let that sensation carry you into tomorrow, and maybe even past that.

Experiences like these often show up when we're at a low point. We could use a jolt of encouragement and *bang!* there's the notice of a position that would be perfect, or the unexpected conversation that cracks open a door. We follow up; our hopes rise. Then that rising shoots out a little spurt of energy that carries us through another couple of days. It's enough to get us to try again. And even if this particular whatever doesn't pan out, it's held a place for us, opened space for the important business of imagining ourselves back at work.

31

Thunder Mountain

When you are looking, hoping, waiting, some days crawl slower than a tortoise. You're watching the clock, checking email every few minutes for some change, calculating how long before lunch.

Other days hurtle along like they're shot out of a gun and you can hardly keep up with the requests for information, the filling out of applications, the breathless calls from friends who just heard about something that would be perfect for you.

Which of these is more common? Which more accurately reflects life as you know it? Which do you prefer?

And what if it's not a matter of either/or, but both/and? Meaning, that slow and fast, anticipation and activity, rattling around and falling headlong out of control are all part of the reality in this in between time.

It's like you're living in an amusement park, stuck on the roller coaster. One moment you're climbing, slowly, oh so slowly. The next, you're dropped off a cliff, arms up, screaming, all smiles.

Bear in mind that many gladly pay good money and wait hours for this sort of experience.

32

Dream on

Some people are in between because the notion of a cubicle, or answering to a boss, or punching a clock makes their hands shake and their lips numb. They are artists; they are musicians; they are inventors; they are farmers; they are writers; they are protesters; they are confident of life lived along a different path.

They are, in a word, dreamers.

If this is you, wonderful! And if you can make it go—if you can manage life where your dream gets food to the table, coffee in the carafe, and gas in the tank—marvelous!

And if this was you—or will be you, one day—and now other concerns are rising to the point where you're giving them attention, then please: Do not despair. The fire in which dreams are forged is often plenty hot enough to propel you towards what you need to keep life and limb intact. And as you find yourself on this path, know that you're likely to find company.

At the same time, you may need to make adjustments to accommodate your dream—like maybe a part-time gig that pulls down enough dough to pay the bills while you continue to build that stairway to heaven. That's been the pattern for plenty: they work two (or more) jobs until the one they love most dearly is big enough to carry them year-round. Between here and there, though, a lot of them also discover exhaustion. But it's a good exhaustion.

It helps that you're creative, too, because that will come in handy. Creativity is a huge plus when it comes to finding ways to stock the fridge and stay warm (or cool). Don't be surprised, though, if you find yourself scrambling. And, don't bail too soon.

Don't complain, either. If you're choosing this life, embrace it. If you do find yourself complaining about more than enjoying this life, however, that may be a signal that a change is worth considering. Struggling dreamers are no problem—they can even be endearing. Bitter, whiny dreamers? Nobody wants them around at brunch.

33

A prayer to start the day

That Your glory rises in the morning sun
and sparkles off flowing waters,
that the glory of the everlasting world
shines in this world
growing from the ground and issuing forth
from every creature,
that glory can be handled, seen, and known
in the matter of earth and human relationships
and the most ordinary matters of daily life–
assure me again this day, O God,
assure me again this day.

J. Phillip Newell

▸

34

Path to great

> *... whoever wants to be great among you must be your servant*
> Mark 10:43

Jesus' statement is prompted by a question from James and John. Can *we* be great? they ask. Sure, says Jesus. All it takes is a walk down *this* road. Are you ready for that?

One of the wonderful gifts of this in between time *is* time—hours and days absent the pressure of urgent demands. Not that there aren't things to take care of, even now. But there is less that must be done. And in such a season, we can, if we are intentional about it, pause to reflect.

One question to ask: Do I want to be great? Not: noticed, famous, wealthy, powerful—but great. Then the follow up: Am I willing to accept Jesus' definition of greatness, *and* His strategy for achieving it?

The in between time reminds us that we can't always lead, can't always be in charge, can't always exert our will. When we face that, we can also see, however, that opportunities to serve are never absent.

35

Lest we settle

Early on in the search, we expect and look for the same sort of job we left. A ways into it, we imagine a better job. After more time passes, we lower our sights and widen our parameters.

Funny, how this can parallel our 'spiritual life'. Over time, enthusiasm can cool, and we're willing to do with, willing to expect, less.

Sir Francis Drake's prayer for spiritual revival stirs us from complacency:

> Disturb us, Lord, when we are too pleased with ourselves,
> When our dreams have come true because we dreamed too little,
> When we arrived safely because we sailed too close to the shore.
> Disturb us, Lord, when with the abundance of things we possess
> We have lost our thirst
> for the waters of life;

Having fallen in love with life,
we have ceased to dream of eternity
And in our efforts to build a new earth,
we have allowed our vision
Of the new Heaven to dim.
Disturb us, Lord, to dare more boldly,
To venture on wilder seas where storms will show Your mastery;
Where losing sight of land,
we shall find the stars.
We ask you to push back the horizons of our hopes;
And to push back the future in strength, courage, hope, and love.
This we ask in the name of our Captain, who is Jesus Christ.

May our horizons not narrow too soon. ▸

36

Hang on

Self-focus is a temptation during this season. That is, the situation we're in seems larger than anything else around us, to the point where it consumes us. We stop noticing others, stop caring in meaningful ways.

A line from the New Testament book of Hebrews (Encourage one another—and all the more as you see the Day approaching... *Hebrews 10:25*) shakes us out of this by reminding us of two things.

First, that "the Day" is approaching. The day of Jesus' return, the writer of Hebrews means; the day when God's rule is fully established. This writer wants us to keep looking up and out, to a coming day that will usher us into a new era. This doesn't mean today is irrelevant, or that 'these days' don't matter. Rather, it's that our present day should not overwhelm us, or lure us into thinking this is all there is.

Second, with the call to "encourage one another," we're supposed to be mindful of those around us. A tricky business, this—because our own situation (*I'm out of work!*) can suck most of the air out of any room. We might notice others in our peripheral vision, but mostly thought and energy revolves around *me*.

Trouble is, such an orientation left unchecked poisons our souls and the communities we're part of. So, while it's true that we who are among the unemployed need encouragement, it's also the case that others around us—those with jobs, friends, spouses, parents, kids, bills, illness, potential—all these folks could stand some encouragement, too.

Today, that's your job.

37

Facing big problems

In an interview with Bill Moyers, Wendell Berry talked about the misguided effort of trying to tackle big problems with easy solutions. Berry said that we're quick to impose our will on what troubles us, using brute force on what we think needs changing or fixing. We move in fast; we come down hard.

A better approach, Berry suggests, is to start with curiosity. Ask questions. Wait and see what might unfold.

During the interview, this philosopher farmer was talking about sociological and political tensions that affect wide swaths of people and systems. But his comments also scale to smaller spheres, because individuals face significant setbacks, too.

Take Berry's observation that solutions to big problems are rarely easy or quick. Noticing the prevailing tendency when faced with trouble to respond with force, or withdraw altogether, or expect to find the right lever to pull, Berry instead counsels patience. In the interview, he was commending the strategy to governments—but it's surprisingly effective in your house, and in mine.

Wendell Berry acknowledges that when things are bad—when they need changing or fixing, or when there is an emergency—curiosity and patience don't seem all that interesting. But they are, to his mind, essential. ▸

Notice this

When you have a good day, when someone says something that lifts your spirits, when the rusted bolt loosens, when you stumble upon a great sale, when you spot a beautiful flower, when you smell running water, when supper is marvelous, when you hear God in a hymn or your heart—notice that.

Let it lodge, and linger. Write it down. Tell someone else.

Hammer it like a piton into the rock wall you are climbing. ▶

39

The gallery

Are you hearing voices?

You know what I mean: words, phrases, accusations laid against you by people who knew or know you. Those who feel a need to speak into your life, but who do so in ways that erode confidence and gnaw at your soul. *Those* voices.

Me, too.

Some speak from the distant past. I hail from a line of no-nonsense Swiss and Germans (pictures of ancestors collected and catalogued by my brother show not a jester among them) who labored diligently and, according to stories passed down, wanted the same from those around them. If we had a family crest, *Work Hard* would be the motto.

Others are more recent. In my early years of church work, for instance, a few parishioners added criticism and downright meanness to the *Do more!* I inherited. It was *The Muppets'* Statler and Waldorf without the comedy, and these hecklers gave me a playlist that blares out more often than I'd like.

Thankfully, there have been other voices, too. Friends, mentors, acquaintances, and even a number of relatives have offered kind words and humor often and at key moments.

Who speaks to/yells at you? To whom do you listen? What voices matter?

We have something to say about who sits in the balcony of our hearts and minds. We can reserve seats for cantankerous Muppets, and maybe figure out some way of dealing with their taunts and jeers. But what if instead we assemble a crowd like the one at the end of *Rudy*, when young Samwise Gamgee breaks through the offensive line to sack the QB? Schmaltzy, sure—but if you're surrounded by peeps like his, get ready for a pretty good run.

40

Take a break

Since you're not on the clock, every day can feel like a weekend. Or, if you're nervous about finding a new position, or trying to do every last thing you can think of as well as what those around you suggest, every day is too short and you see absolutely no point or sense in taking time off.

If either of these sounds familiar, you might be ready for a Sabbath.

I know: *Sabbath* sounds like an old-fashioned idea, a quaint custom from back when computers were the size of battleships. And yet, Sabbath is one of those ideas the Bible recommends in several places: it's one of the ten shaping words brought down from Sinai by Moses; prophets insist upon it; even Jesus assumes those who love and follow God will embrace Sabbath.

Perhaps it would help to think of Sabbath as more than just the day you're supposed to go to church. From there, try broadening your view to the point that Sabbath is for changing up the normal pace of things. Use it to enjoy the fruit of labor. Welcome Sabbath as a day when you take a break from trying to solve problems.

This might sound ridiculous, I know. When you're out of work, problems crop up at every point on the compass. But stay with me for a minute.

Sabbath is meant to be part of the routine we adopt for a virtuous life—one where our values are patterned after God's. As such, it reminds us that a healthy rhythm includes both work and rest, both bearing down and easing off.

Taken like this, Sabbath isn't a vacation to which we're entitled; it's one more part of the life we're building. We need it, the way we need food, or air. And it's good for us, too, like mountain vistas and early mornings in a tree stand. ▸

41

Anxious

"Anxiety" in my vocabulary means a kind of fretfulness that occupies mental bandwidth and tips me toward emotional fatigue. It has typically been full of negative connotations. So imagine my surprise when I found Diana Butler Bass's words on this word:

> Anxiety is frequently the mark of personal transformation, for anxiety is a primary emotion when the heart feels disoriented and lost. Indeed, awakenings and the backlash they spawn may not happen with great regularity, but when they do happen to individuals and societies, great tension and division is a normal (if disconcerting) part of the process of spiritual and cultural revitalization.

Anxiety as part of "personal transformation," or societal awakenings? Of course, these remarks come in the larger context of change. Will we, Bass asks, when we stand at the edge of a new idea or practice or possibility and sense an inner turmoil (because we are, while peering over that ledge, anxious), step back to alleviate the sensation? That is, will the presence of that feeling keep us from moving into what might actually be really, really good?

Bass says that such feelings are normal for those who face the unknown. But she goes on to encourage moving into the change responsible for that anxiety, rather than automatically shunning it.

Change is, by its nature, new, a disruption of the status quo and therefore destabilizing; anxiety is a reasonable response to it. But: anxiety need not make us run the other way. Rather, as we face change, and all that accompanies it, we can pause, name what's going on, and take whatever time and heart is required to determine whether what we're feeling is there to keep us from danger, or simply because we're stepping into the unknown—where (who knows?) something glorious may be lurking. ▸

42

Either/Or

A mid-afternoon break morphed into a philosophical moment when I opened a bar of Green & Black's *Maya Gold*. There, inside the cover, I read, in faint grey type, the company logo: *Living in the &.*

Living in the &?

In an age when binary thinking (black/white; right/wrong; my way/the highway) is so common, the encouragement of this company is refreshing (they make pretty good chocolate, too). A good reminder as we barrel along that lots of people have ideas, that lots of ideas bear more careful consideration, that notions or concepts we're prone to disagree with can (occasionally, at least) hold a nugget worth pondering.

Hooray, then, for chocolate (of course) and wise confectioners who nudge us out past . and ! into the height, width, and depth of &

43

The way you tell it

I lost my job…

or

During this time between jobs, I've been thinking carefully about my strengths, interests, and objectives. I'm honing a skill that hasn't yet received the time it deserved. I'm recovering from a season of significant stress. I'm checking possibilities, following leads, interacting with a wide and generous network. I'm praying for peace, clarity, and patience—and remembering the amazing ways God has come through. And while I stumble over this one occasionally, I'm trying to see each day as a gift.

Both descriptions are true. Each leads to a different place.

Where are you going?

44

Pushing water uphill

> The difficult can be done immediately.
> The impossible takes a little longer.
> *Motto of the US Army Corp of Engineers*

Most days in between are challenging, for one reason or another. In the initial weeks or months of this season, you notice this; you might even remark on it to those within earshot. As more time passes, however, you discover that the level of difficulty hasn't changed a great deal—but your attitude about it has.

This is worth pondering.

Shifts like this happen when people give up or cave in—when they resign themselves to another mindless circuit round the sun during which nothing will change. Is this you?

Another way to explain the shift is that you're stronger now than when this season began. That is, you've walked this road long enough to become familiar with its twists and turns. You've accepted—deliberately—the path you're on. Your stamina has increased; you're even noticing the flora and fauna around you. Not that you wouldn't take a different route (if a position you're seeking came open, you'd say yes) but you've made peace with this one.

Those outside your situation and looking in are surprised by your equanimity. Sometimes, *you* are surprised by your equanimity. But there it is: you're managing. You're discovering that "difficult" is relative. You're even thinking "impossible" isn't outside the pale, either.

45

Worry more

More worrying will bring peace.

Worry is the best and quickest way of getting where you want to go.

It is good for friends and family to worry often and deeply about your situation.

Spend most of today worrying. Fill any extra time with being pessimistic.

Worry promotes good sleep and provides extra energy when you're awake.

Worry shows how seriously you're taking this in between time.

Some of us need to be tricked into walking away from what's harmful. If that's you, imagine a series of epithets or commands that advocate what you're having trouble resisting (like worry). Then ask: How long does it take before this sounds ridiculous? ▸

46

Don't forget

When this season ends, don't forget the people who walked with you.

Don't forget all God did in, around, through, and for you.

Don't forget what you've learned, or how you acquired that knowledge.

And, don't forget there are others who are still in between. Call them. Take them out for coffee. Have them over for a meal. Find some work for them to do—even if it's only a couple of hours cleaning, painting, babysitting, or moving furniture—and pay them. Ask your friends to hire them, too. Loan them something. Make it possible for them to enjoy a luxury. Pray for them. Listen to them. Go back, and listen some more. Remind them that you think highly of them—that being 'out of work' is not a reason for shame. Assure them that all will be well.

47

Remember

A card from a friend came in the mail one day. It carried a 'front and center' message for the in between times. ▸

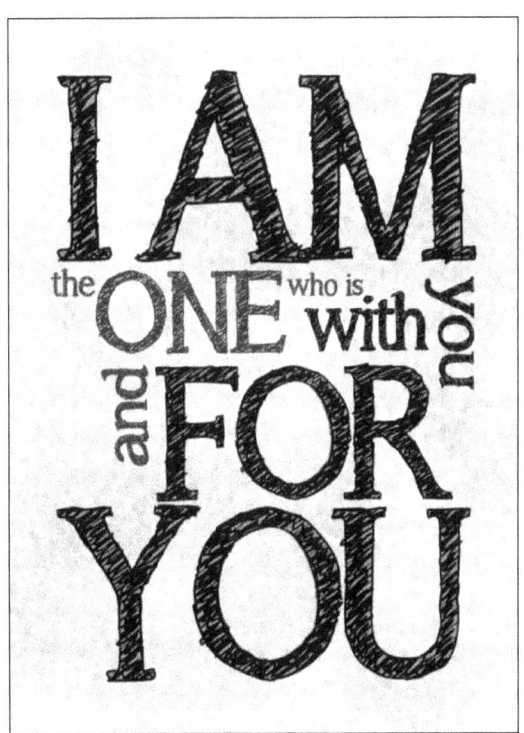

Notes

Chapter

22 This writer, Carol Merritt Howard, wrote "Fired? Forced out? You're not alone," September 29, 2014, http://www. christiancentury.org/blogs/arc hive/%252Ffired-forced-out-youre-not-alone.

29 During the rebuilding of Jerusalem's walls after the exile to Babylon, Nehemiah says that "we prayed to our God and posted a guard" (Nehemiah 4:9). It's a nice juxtaposition of waiting on the Lord, even while doing something.

33 The Friday morning prayer of J. Phillip Newell, in *Sounds of the Eternal: A Celtic Psalter* (Grand Rapids, MI: Eerdmans, 2002), p. 65.

35 I'm indebted to J. B. Wood for alerting me to this in *At Work As It Is In Heaven: 25 Ways to Reimagine the Spiritual Purpose of Your Work* (Patheos Press, 2012).

37 Bill Moyers' interview of Wendell Berry is at http://billmoyers.com /episode/full-show-wendell-berry-poet-prophet/

38 In Psalm 97:11 (*Light shines on the righteous and joy on the upright in heart*), I hear the idea that light and joy are not just qualities or blessings we're born with, but also gifts from "the Most High" to use and relish.

40 John H. Walton, *The Lost World of Genesis One: Ancient Cosmology and the Origins Debate* (Downers Grove, IL: IVP Academic, 2009), p. 73.

41 Diana Butler Bass, *Christianity After Religion: The End of Church and the Birth of a New Spiritual Awakening* (New York: Harper One, 2012), p. 250f.

45 Thanks to Rebecca Adams who inspired this one.

47 Margot Starbuck designed this image using a translation of the Hebrew term *YHWH*.

Prompts
for continued reflection
and further discussion

The questions and nudges on these next pages are tied to chapters in this book; some prompts include Scripture to read, too. While you can certainly go through them on your own, they can also guide discussion and consideration by small groups.

Another suggestion:
Don't feel compelled to interact with all of these prompts. There are enough that you can choose what is of interest, and what fits your particular situation.

.1.

Theme: Shame

Connected chapters: 6, 7, 13, 39

To consider:
Shame is a common feeling for those who are in between. But, is this justified?

Take a moment or two to think/talk about why and how the culture you're in shames people.

Try to identify why *you* might be feeling shame—list some reasons for this.

Now ask:
(1) How much of the shame you feel comes from believing that others see—or ought to see—you in a particular way?

(2) How many of these reasons are your fault? That is, what have you done to bring shame on yourself?

(3) With respect to (2), how much of this can be put away by making an apology, or shifting an attitude? What happens if you acknowledge what

you've done, and deal with it? Can you release shame?

(4) What will it take to reframe your story in a way that is true, and where 'failure' is neither the starting nor the main point of your self-description?

Scripture to read:
Psalm 8
Habakkuk 3:19
John 8:2-11
1 Corinthians 1:26-30

.2.

Theme: A day in the life

Connected chapters: 4, 7, 17, 18, 29, 42

To consider:
Pick a recent day during this in between time and go through it in blocks of 2-3 hours, from when you woke up to when you went back to bed. What did you do in these periods of time? How did you feel during them? Be as specific as you can.

Look over that list of activity and feelings. How much of it is different from a typical day when you're working at a 'real' job?

How much of it seems perfectly reasonable in light of your current situation?

What parts of your day are you most proud of? Why?

What's missing from your days that might otherwise be beneficial? What would it take to add some of that to tomorrow?

Scripture to read:
Psalm 90
Matthew 5:1-16
1 Peter 4:10

.3.

Theme: Helping helpers

Connected chapters: 1, 9, 16, 36, 43

To consider:
List some of the things people say to you, or ask you about, during this season.

As you look over that list, note lines you hear and questions you're asked that are encouraging. Use a second notation for statements and queries that annoy you.

What's the difference between your two lists?

Can you imagine showing these lists to friends and family members as a way of discussing what you need—and what is of benefit—while you're in between?

.4.

Theme: Sabbath/Rest

Connected chapters: 1, 33, 40

To consider:
In *The Lost World of Genesis One*, John Walton talks about Day 7—the Sabbath—as the climax of the creation story. That is, he suggests seeing Sabbath not as the end so much as the peak of God's activity. Walton points out that

> ...in the ancient world, rest is what results when a crisis has been resolved or when stability has been achieved–when things have 'settled down'. Consequently, normal routines can be established and enjoyed.... This is more a matter of engagement without obstacles than disengagement without responsibilities. (73)

With that last line, Walton looks at Sabbath as an opportunity to live with what has been accomplished. For six days, we attend to "obstacles" (what we might in our context call "work"); on the seventh, we change our focus.

Walton offers a lens that focuses first on the 'work week'—which is full of "obstacles" (problems to solve, responsibilities to fulfill, water to push uphill)—and then on the Sabbath. He reminds us that this seventh day is a gift (see Jesus' support of that in Mark 2:27). Sabbath offers the opportunity to step back and enjoy what the work has made possible.

Precisely how we fill Sabbath varies from person to person. While many have, for good reason, connected it with gathered worship, there are other ways of spending Sabbath, as well.

Take some time to talk and think about the 'content' of Sabbath—particularly in terms of "engagement without obstacles."

Another matter to ponder: might Sabbath be a time to 'reset' what has been overrun by other concerns, commitments, and/or obligations? If so, what does that involve?

Scripture to read:
Exodus 20:8
Mark 2:23-28

.5.

Theme: God is still speaking

Connected chapters: 11, 12, 34, 38, 47

To consider:
As you're working your way through the injustices you've suffered, and/or the very real pressures of a reduced income and hits to your ego, can you pause long enough to listen for what God may have to say to you?

Try setting aside a few minutes for attending to God.
- Go to a quiet place, or take a walk where you won't be distracted by neighbors or overly friendly wildlife.
- Bring a journal and a reliable pen. Record ideas about what you need to do (when these come to mind, jot them down and then let them go) as well as words, phrases, and impressions that you sense may be coming from the Lord.
- Turn this last point (see above) over in your mind. Pray these items back to the Lord, asking: is this what you want from or in me?

- Do you see the face or hear the name of a person you need to love or forgive?
- Does a phrase or verse or section of Scripture come to mind?

God is still speaking.

What is God saying to you? Think about someone you trust—someone who cares for you and your situation—and ask if you can talk with that person about what has shown up after your time of intentional listening.

.6.

Theme: Fear

Connected chapters: 5, 8, 13, 28, 41, 45

To consider:
In one of Baz Luhrmann's lesser known films—*Strictly Ballroom*—a character wails at a critical moment: "We lived our lives in fear!" The movie is a comedy, but this line perceptively, poignantly expresses the tragedy of being under fear's thumb.

Has fear gripped your life, or a portion thereof? Can you get to the root of that fear? Can you imagine life without fear coiling around your heart?

One of God's great gifts is peace—which comes as a direct opponent to fear. Try listening for that word from God. And if that sounds too weird or difficult, ask a friend who knows and loves God to pray for peace over you.

Here's another idea. Look at your surroundings and schedule, to see if there's too much noise, or too many scary things going on. Decide to do something today that is inherently peaceful: bake, read, listen to music, walk outside, waltz.

Scripture to read:
Psalm 27
Psalm 56
John 14:27

.7.

Theme: The past

Connected chapters: 15, 20, 22, 24

To consider:
How good is your memory? Do you tend to recall past events in great detail? Would others say your recollections are accurate? Do certain things stay with you—even if generally, your memory isn't all that terrific? If so, what lingers? Any chance it's something bad that happened to you, or something another person said that stung?

What does holding on to that memory do to the world you live in?

In Romans 12:17-21, Paul says we're not to repay evil for evil. That is, if someone has hurt us, we don't think about revenge. Instead, we look for ways to extend kindness. Counter-intuitive, to be sure—but life giving.

To emphasize his point, Paul draws from the Proverbs what sounds like a curious image: "In doing this, you will heap burning coals on his head" (Proverbs 25:22). Paul is not suggesting a novel way of getting back at someone, but rather is recalling a very ordinary feature of life at a time and place without electricity or modern convenience.

If the fire one uses to cook or heat with goes out, there's trouble ahead. And so Paul is saying that if you see or know someone who's having this problem, share some of your burning coals with that person.

In other words? Be willing—eager, even—about bringing comfort, doing good to one who has done you wrong.

What happens if you live in a world like that?

Try setting aside a few minutes for attending to God. Be open to ways you may need to offer forgiveness.

Scripture to read:
Ephesians 4:25-27
Colossians 3:12-17

.8.

Theme: Getting ready for what's next

Connected chapters: 23, 31, 35, 46

To consider:
This season will, sooner or later, end. Exactly when that happens may not be clear, but a change is coming.

What will it take to get ready for that?

What might you wish you had done (like house repairs, travel, time with friends, books to read, run a half-marathon, and so on) that you haven't already paid attention to?

With thanks...

Friends scattered across several states and continents have offered support and encouragement during my own in-between times as they have occurred. I'm grateful for each one in this network of compassion.

In this most recent season, several have been especially thoughtful, and I remember them here: Chuck, Mike & Lynne, Crystal & David, Larry & Elaine, Rich, Jane, Don & Babe, Carl, Jonathan & Cathleen, Brett & Marilyn, Kevin & Ann, Grace & Brian, Paul & Cathy, Mark, John, Sharon & Keith, Meg, Tom, Dave & Belinda, and Martha.

And family? Again, I'm blessed by members of a far-flung tribe who call, visit, pray, and cheer.

Other books by Dan Schmidt

Unexpected Wisdom

Studies in the Old Testament's Minor Prophets, where ancient words carry surprisingly contemporary significance

"In their visions, writings, and lives, the Minor Prophets saw and forcefully communicated God's wisdom in radical and unsettling words for their age and culture. Dan Schmidt brings today's readers into the picture by reminding us that the issues the prophets addressed are still with us.... In this penetrating book, God's wisdom for our own lives of faith is spelled out with clarity and compassion.

Luci Shaw, author,
Water My Soul and *The Angels of Light*

Taken by Communion

Paul's description of and meditation on the Eucharist in 1 Corinthians 11 is examined phrase by phrase

"In a world where churches are under pressure to install drive-through lanes, Dan Schmidt calls us to give ourselves to communion as we were meant to—slowly. We're reminded that true communion can become something we don't simply consume, but that consumes us.

John Ortberg, Teaching Pastor,
Menlo Park Presbyterian Church

Letters to Me
A collection of poignant, humorous, insightful essays from respected writers addressing their younger selves

"There is something maddeningly compelling about this book. You want to leap into its pages and shake some sense into the characters just like you're reading a page-turning novel, except that it's real life and if you could somehow grab them by their shoulders, you would realize you were staring yourself in the face. The talent of these storytellers is revealed in how universal their personal stories are. In their stories you will experience agony and joy, pain and healing, fall and redemption.

Adam S. McHugh, author
Introverts in the Church

"One of the most unnerving, unsettling things one can do in life is stare at themselves in the mirror—eye to eye. *Letters To Me* is the sacred chance to witness person after person pause their present as they stand naked in the mirror, facing everything they've been and everything they've done. To listen to what they hear in their souls, to see their past as they truly do. Oh, how I wish I'd been given this collection of stories earlier in my life. The entrance into adulthood would have been painted with so much more grace.

Lauren Lankford Dubinsky,
founder of Good Women Project

::

More information at www.toucanic.net

FICTION

Playa Perdida
When life goes south,
sometimes you need a beach

Prime Target
Soft-boiled crime novel about insurance investigators on a chase, unrequited love, and a bomb

University of Days
(forthcoming 2015)
A year in the life of a southern school where people with mixed motives make important discoveries

FOR CHILDREN (AND GRANDPARENTS)

Hug in a Mug
Everyone knows what Benny needs…

⁂

More information at www.toucanic.net
Books available at Amazon.com

www.ingramcontent.com/pod-product-compliance
Lightning Source LLC
Chambersburg PA
CBHW051807170526
45167CB00005B/1916